adventure

adventure

Christmas poems by Mark Greene

Muddy
Pearl

Published by Muddy Pearl Books,
Edinburgh, Scotland
www.muddypearl.com
books@muddypearl.com

Some of these poems were first published
by Lion Hudson in 1995 in the collection
Opening Night.

British Library Cataloguing in Publication Data.
A catalogue record for this book is available
from the British Library

ISBN 978-1-910012-18-5

Typeset and designed
by RevoCreative
www.revocreative.co.uk

Printed and bound in
Latvia by Livonia Print

Image copyright shutterstock: p10: McCarthy's PhotoWorks, p12: leonello calvetti, p14: udra11, p16: CoolKengzz, p22:
Petar Paunchev, p24: LukaTDB, p26: xpixel, p28: CristinaMuraca, p30: Cafe Racer, p32: Jakub Krechowicz, p34: voljurij,
p36: Background Land, p38: Yuriy Kulik, p40: Vadim Sadovski, p42: Yarygin, p44: Kondrachov Vladimir, p46: BMJ, p48:
Annette Shaff, p54: braedostok, p56: conrado, p58: Johan Larson, p62: Dima Sobko, p64: donsimon, p66: Ana Martinez
de Mingo, p72: Nyvlt-art, p74: Stokkete, p76: Macrovector, p78: jeep5d, p80: Benoit Daoust, p82: KN, p84: Nejron Photo,
p86: Kesu, p90: jokerpro, p92: Zastolskiy Victor, p94: Byjeng, p96: Galyna Andrushko, p98: Sergey Karpov, p102: William
Perugini, p104: ouh_desire, p106: sematadesign, p108: M. Pellinni

For Adam,
my brother,
a man of endless kindness and joy.
With love.

Coming home
for Christmas

Every year I come back to Christmas like a traveller returning home after a year away in a foreign land.

I know this place.

And I am pleased to be here. The pictures on the walls are familiar – like the people and the events in the Christmas story. I am enriched, comforted by the old things. But I see new things, and see the old things in new ways. I have changed, I am changing. We all are. Ideas surface, gleam and take flight.

Christmas, the Christmas that is not about the bubbly frenzy of all the preparations for the big day, still retains its shimmering mystery: ordinary people caught up in the divine drama that is the hinge of history. They are invited to take part, as we are; seeking, as we can; choosing, as we do; pressured, as we are; afraid, exhilarated, and, in the end, grateful, awed, content.

Here the poems, the illustrations, the reflections, and indeed the quotations from the Biblical accounts which inspire them all, combine, we hope, to bring to life some of the myriad facets of the birth of the one who came to change our world, and us, and still does today.

Contents

01

Gravity

Gravity

The apple, unlike Adam, had no choice but to fall,
Speeding to fulfil its Creator's call.
But what force drew him down to us?
He, with a starlit infinity to explore,
He, who could peer into a neutron's core,
He, who had spoken a thousand million times
And known the sulphuric spit of our self-vaunting crimes,
He, whom we had called murderer, liar, thief,
And left for dead with enlightened relief.

What force drew him down from above
To reap the grim harvest of rebel pride,
Hammered with nails of truth denied?
What force drew him down from above?
What force but this: the gravity of love.

01

For God so loved the world that he gave his one and only Son,
that whoever believes in him shall not perish but have eternal life.

JOHN 3:16

Fruit had been
falling off trees for billions
of years but gravity was only
discovered in 1687. Things can be there
without our understanding them. And
things can be there without our noticing.
The neutron was discovered in 1932, the
quark in 1968 and Higgs boson only
confirmed in 2012. We learn more,
and wonderfully discover there is
more to learn.

02

Zechariah
& the Angel

Zechariah & the Angel

Afterwards he would have time aplenty to ponder
That it is perhaps not politic, nor even polite,
Nor even quite sane,
To question divine omnipotence
With an angel staring you in the face.

But you can grow too used to empirical evidence:
That month on month longing for news of blood's absence,
She and he bleeding on, moon after moon,
The wound of longing unstaunched, the public stain,
Clear from her flat belly, the both bearing the heavy bulge
Of imputed shame, mulling the enigma of God's favour,
Apparently withheld, hope on the wane...
'Til
Aching age replaces anguished youth,
And blood's absence becomes an ever-present banner
Of barrenness vanquished by impossibility,
The season surely for common sense.

Yes, you can grow too used to hard evidence,
Even with an angel staring you in the face.

Both of them were righteous in the sight of God, observing all the Lord's commands and decrees blamelessly. But they were childless because Elizabeth was not able to conceive, and they were both very old.

LUKE 1:6–7

Infertility is an agony for any couple in any age and easily interpreted as divine disfavour, as sadly are other misfortunes, adding spiritual guilt and social shame to anguished disappointment.

17

03

The Offer

The Offer

It was an offer she could have refused,
A life she could have used
In some other way.
To grow great with child, for example,
After her wedding day;
To forego the knowing looks
and the slur of slut;
To defer to another the chance
to tell a father
And watch the word twist in her fiance's gut;
To make room for some noble's daughter
To carry the cause of innocents' slaughter;
To allow some other to cradle a son
Pale from his pinioned death.

She could have said:
'All things considered,
And though I am flattered,
I would rather not.
I am just a village girl,
Not fit for such matters.'

Of course, there was the
sigh of angel's wings,
The words with all his promises
ripened for now,
The chance to do something extraordinary,
To let what was ordinary become...
But afterwards would it not seem
such girlish fancy?

She, turning from the safety
Of merely human possibility,
Marvelling at how could it be,
That he should choose her to bless,
Welcomed truth to her womb, and said,
'Yes.'

In the sixth month of Elizabeth's pregnancy, God sent the angel Gabriel to Nazareth, a town in Galilee, to a virgin pledged to be married to a man named Joseph, a descendant of David. The virgin's name was Mary.

LUKE 1:26–27

The average age of first pregnancy in the UK is 30, as it is in contemporary Israel. In first century Israel it was probably 16. With over 33,000 teenagers giving birth in 2013, the UK had the highest rate of any Western European nation.

04

The Trip

The Trip

It was not doubt
That took her on the road.
The angel's words did not fade
With the passing of days.
No, it was not doubt
That made her exclaim
The question the sceptics
Would pose again and again:
'How can it be, and I a virgin still?'
Not doubt, more an amazed joy
That soared above the shout of shame.

It was not doubt
That took her to the hills,
More a zealous curiosity
To see for herself
How he was working it out,

To skip in the track of each new step,
To laugh at the mound of evidence,
Elizabeth's baby swelling her dress,
Confounding the critics' common sense:
'How can it be, and she beyond the age?'
To learn that the child leapt in the womb
Just at their presence in the room.
To hear from someone she could trust,
Who knew that hers was not the bloom
Of some undiscovered, earthly lust,
That through her labour would come rest,
Mercy after such insistence at the breast,
Heaven from this tiny, terrestrial guest.

How can it be, how can it be?

04

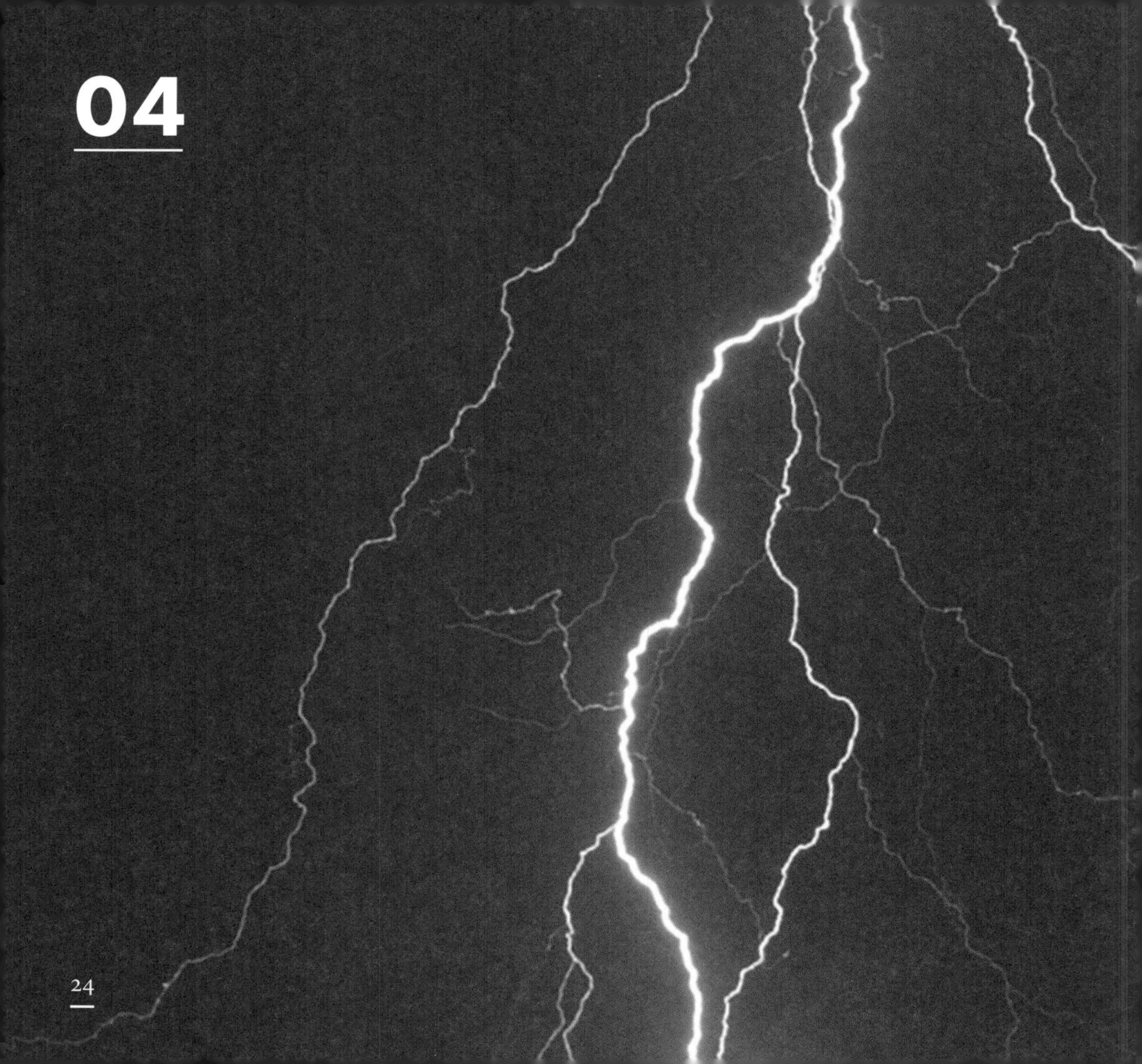

fewer people go to church these days, but more of us, research shows, believe that we have seen angels, have had answers to prayer and perceive some higher power shaping our personal destiny. Miracle and mystery pervade the universe. The believer cries out in awed wonder at the God who can do impossible things and many of those not so sure still wonder in awe. And wonder often leads to wondering. Even in a sceptical age, the intimation of the supernatural cannot be suppressed.

At that time Mary got ready and hurried to a town in the hill country of Judea, where she entered Zechariah's home and greeted Elizabeth.

LUKE 1:39–40

05

First John

First John

John was the first to know,
Tucked up in the womb,
No bigger than an avocado,
When Mary entered the room.

He, having no breath to call 'Attention',
To the High King of all creation,
Small as a mustard seed in the virgin's belly,
Leapt like a gazelle against the soft insides,
A wordless halleluiah of delighted surprise.
And heard his mother's booming reply,
And Mary's words soaring like starlings to
the sky.

That was where he learned
That the darkness
Cannot keep out the light;
That faith comes by spirit
And not by sight;
That a son can be ahead
Of his mother;
That one testimony
Can lead to another.

Later people would ask him when it began.
The truth is: he was always Jesus' man.

05

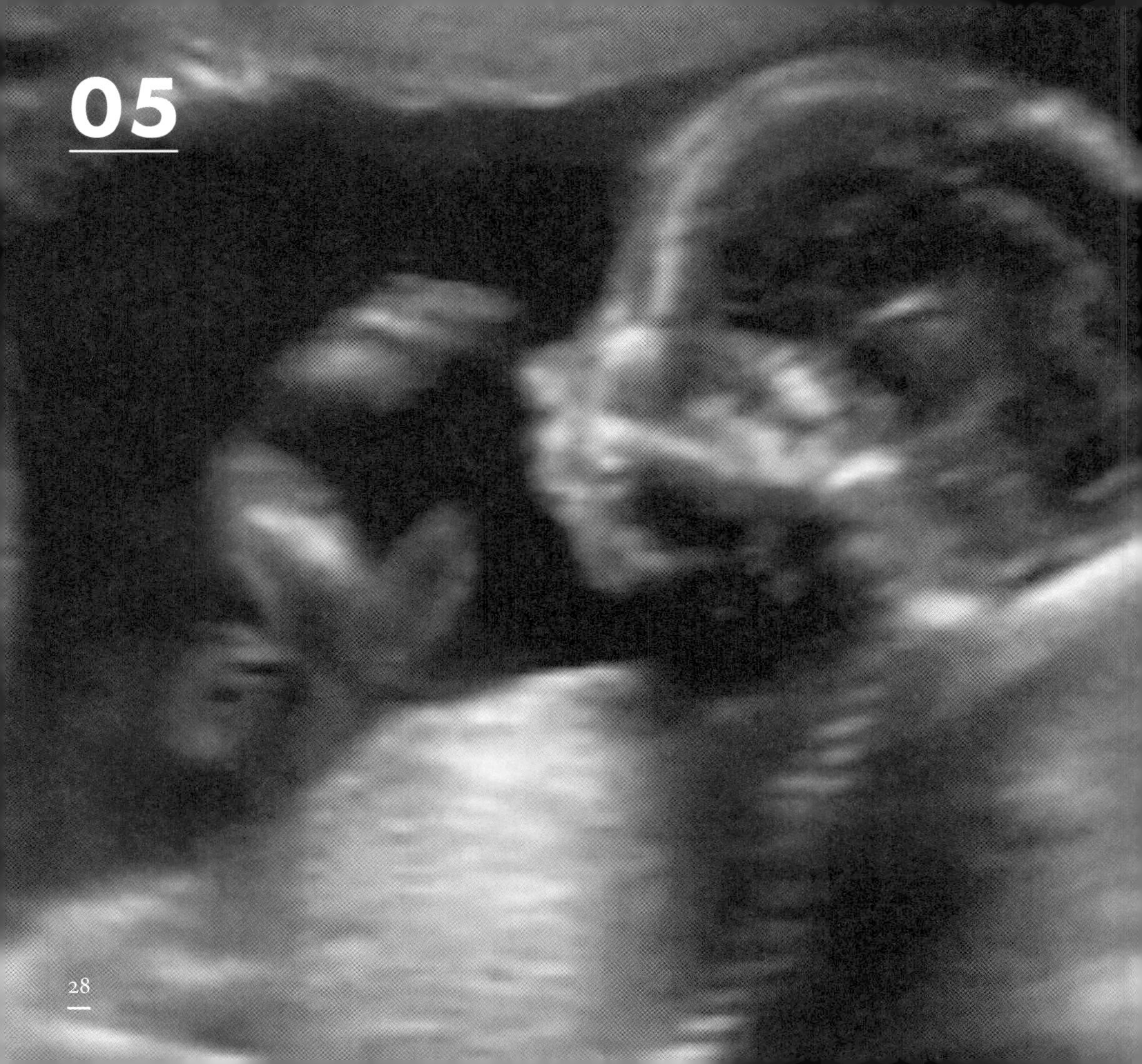

When Elizabeth heard Mary's greeting, the baby leaped in her womb, and Elizabeth was filled with the Holy Spirit …

LUKE 1:41

John the Baptist, Jesus' cousin, became a hugely influential figure in Israel and beyond. Thousands went into the desert to hear him and we know that years after his death he had followers in places as far away as Ephesus, some 1200 miles from Jerusalem. But celebrity and popularity didn't turn his head. He never saw himself as anything more than a warm-up act, a forthright herald preparing the people

for the Messiah's imminent arrival. Few warm-up acts have ever been so self-effacing, so content to leave the stage, and so clear about the superiority of the one who would follow: 'I am not worthy to untie the thongs of his sandals,' he said. He was imprisoned for denouncing Herod's adultery, and subsequently executed.

06

The Girl
with the
Wings of an
Angel in her
Eyes

The Girl with the Wings of an Angel in her Eyes

What was she expecting,
The girl with the wings of an angel in her eyes?
A child, yes, a son ...
But having known no man in the Biblical sense,
Having no physical father to ponder,
What, she must have wondered,
As mind and stomach stretched,
Might a man, born of divine essence
And sweet obedience,
Resemble?

An angel, a seraph? Or some holy paragon?
With the first Adam's pure fresh gaze?
Jacob's smooth hands, Moses' radiant face,
Or the wavy, raven locks of Solomon
And a body like polished ivory?
How would God manifest his glory?
Could she conceive this son of the most high
Would choose to look really rather ordinary?
Miracles, she would learn, are not all discerned
With the naked eye.

06

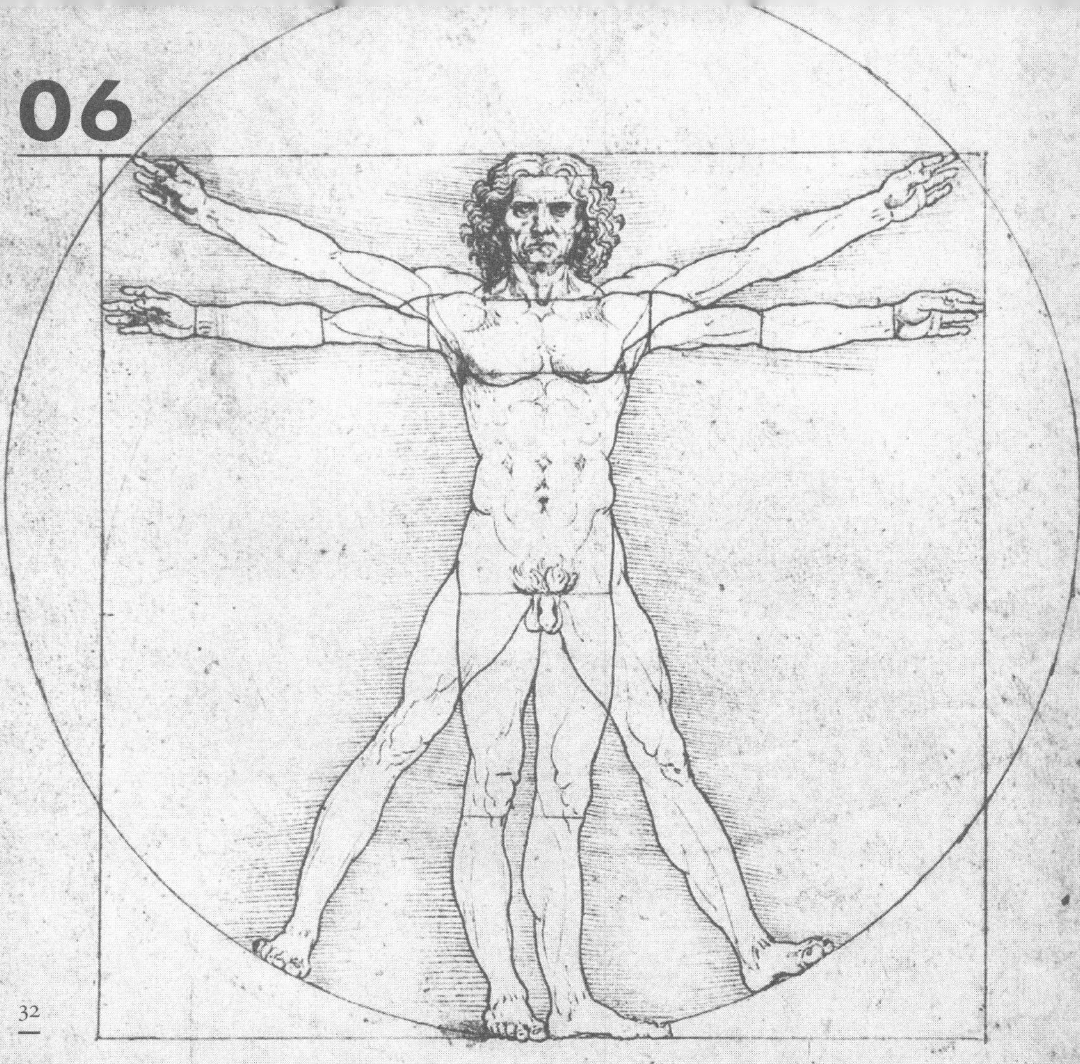

'*… what is conceived in her is from the Holy Spirit.*'

AN ANGEL SPEAKING TO JOSEPH IN A DREAM
MATTHEW 1:20

Our culture is very, very interested in what people look like, and what potions, regimes, foods, accessories and measures they've used to achieve the look. But nowhere in the New Testament does it tell us what Jesus looked like – that he had piercing blue eyes like Robert Powell's Hollywood Jesus, or the aquiline nose of Ted Neeley's Jesus Christ Superstar, or the sculpted torso and groomed locks of Salvador Dali's Christ on a mid-air cross. In fact, we don't know what any of the people in the New Testament looked like. It wasn't important to the writers. Identity was more important than image. There might be a lesson in that.

07

Zechariah's Child

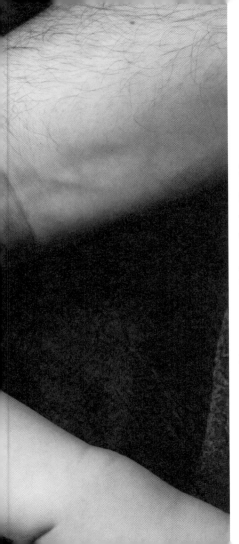

Zechariah's Child

Nine months and more he too was pregnant,
Struck dumb by his own question,
All speech locked inside,
In his long sentence of silence,
A new understanding slowly forming,
Of the miracle he had half descried.
Nine months and more to loosen his grip
On limitation and let truth grow,
Head and heart and hands and feet,
And come alive, warm, pulsing, heavy:
The child, the pledge of a greater dawn,
And Zechariah, crying out with new life,
Nation, world, universe about to be reborn.

Perhaps for each of us there are some lessons we cannot learn, some wisdom we cannot acquire, some perspective we can't see unless we're forced to pause. Zechariah's grace-enforced silence, like the slow aging of a malt whisky in the dark womb of an oak barrel, led to a grand distillation of a universe-transforming vision.

'And now you will be silent and not able to speak until the day this happens, because you did not believe my words, which will come true at their appointed time.'

GABRIEL, THE ANGEL, TO ZECHARIAH
LUKE 1:20

Star Witness

Star Witness

The heavens declare, and though many an eye
Has paused to stare at star-studded sky,
And seen Creator in creation as plain as day,
Still, they never take us quite seriously.
We material objects are thought far too dumb,
Our sensibilities too numb, to utter mystery.

As if we don't have fire in our bellies,
Or an eye that twinkles with delight
In the knowledge of his constant sight.
As if He himself had not said
That the stones themselves would cry out.
What then of we they call dwarves
A hundred times larger than their bright sun,
Should we not have voices to praise the One?

No, you humans, deaf to stone, in time fleeting blips,
Are gone too soon to learn our song or read our lips.
But can any deny my speech was as clear to the Magi
As Philip's, when to Nathanael's questioning heart, he
Gave simple reply: 'Come and see'? Come and see.

The heavens declare the glory of God;
the skies proclaim the work of his hands.
Day after day they pour forth speech;
night after night they reveal knowledge.

DAVID WRITING IN PSALM 19:1-2

The biggest star that has been discovered so far is UY Scuti.
Its radius is 1708 times bigger than our sun and its volume
5 billion times larger. There are some big things out there.
There's no way of being sure from historical records what the
Magi saw — perhaps it was a comet, or perhaps an exploding
supernova, or perhaps …

In a hi-tech multi-media age, when we're used to messages coming to us in a wide range of media, it is perhaps easy to miss just how many different media God uses – from a single angel to a host of them filling the sky, from the words of prophets spoken hundreds of years previously to the words of an 84-year-old woman interpreting the birth of a boy in Bethlehem, from the silent but compelling directing of the spirit to the concrete sign of a child in an animal feeding trough, from dreams to a single star shining in the east. There's no app for all of that.

41

09

Travelling Light

Travelling Light

It wasn't much to go,
You might say,
Obvious enough to the naked eye
But still just one more glimmer
In a glimmering sky.
A clue easily overlooked,
A sign easily passed by
In the bustle of familiar days.

So, they, alone of all those who saw,
set out,
Leaving behind friends who must have
thought them mad:
This time, this time they were going too far,
Just a tad too intense about the rightness of
their view;
And families fearing for their lives
On a long journey to who knew where.
Certainly they didn't,
Having no book to say it was then,
then and there.

So, they, alone in all the world, set out.
A relief it must have been just to be going
and gone...

Almost at the end, up to a king's court,
Seeking some answer to their destination,
His wise men told them precisely where:
Just a few miles down the road.
But the wise did not care

to join them.
Of course, they had seen the star
And the book had told them just where,
But five miles, five miles is just a tad too far.

So, at the start, alone, persuading no one
along the way,
They, who had left friends,
family and sanity behind,
To find: a few animals, a man and his wife,
and in the hay,
A child who had no words to say,
no gifts to bestow,
No way to show his pleasure in
their adoration,
They did not exult that yes,
Yes, all along they had been right
But bowed down, for here,
Here, at last, was the light.

'We saw his star when it rose
and have come to worship him.'

THE MAGI TO KING HEROD
MATTHEW 2:2

The Bible doesn't call Jesus' eastern visitors 'kings' but 'Magi', originally a Persian word that by the first century embraced a range of people interested in dreams, astrology, magic, predictions of the future. Some Magi were no doubt fakes, some deluded, and some genuine seekers of truth.

10

Opening Night

Opening Night

A spotlight locked on a small provincial town.
A shed converted for the purpose.
The steamy breath of animals,
Shuffling at a teenager's cries.
And finally,
A different cry, the sweat mopped away.
The quiet.
The crunch of the straw pressed down.
Her child asleep.

Not many came,
Though this was where they said it would be.
A few out-of-towners from the east,
A handful of nightworkers on the skive.
Not many came
To see this ordinary sight,
The new Life lit by a singular light.

10

When the angels had left them and gone into heaven, the shepherds said to one another, 'Let's go to Bethlehem and see this thing that has happened, which the Lord has told us about.'

LUKE 2:15

I suspect that if I happened to have a host of angels at my disposal to announce the most significant birth in history I wouldn't send them to, for example, the security guards working the night shift on a deserted industrial estate. Back in the first century shepherding was like much night work today – poorly paid and socially excluding. And shepherds were widely regarded with disdain and suspicion. But they hear the history-changing news first. With God, the poor and the marginalised are a priority. And he makes that clear from the start.

11

Out of the Blue...

Out of the Blue...

The historic present.

And future perfect
Concentrated in him,
Infinite love locked in linen.

The answer,

To purpose,
And the ache of the heart
And the clench of the knotted will,

Poised to pour
Fullness,
Cascading
Beyond the brim
Of all we are,

The king
Laying his gifts at our feet.

11

1984. If you were living in East Berlin could you have imagined a life without communism, without the wall? 1960. Soweto. If you were living in that township, could you have imagined a day when not only would there be a black President but when white and black and coloured people would live together in harmony?

Often, when we imagine the future, it's like the present but more so. But history and our own lives teach us that it is not always so.

New York, September 10th, 2001, 9.15am. Could anyone really have imagined that the politics of the world would be so utterly different in 24 hours?

As for the Jews of Israel under Roman occupation in, say, 10 BC, well, they had for centuries hoped for the arrival of a saviour, a Messiah. He had been long predicted but was not imminently expected but then, out of the blue... God had been working in an unfashionable northern town, far from the madding crowd, in the lives of an apparently ordinary young woman and a village carpenter... And their lives and the course of all human history were about to change.

NOW FAITH IS CONFIDENCE IN WHAT WE HOPE FOR AND ASSURANCE ABOUT WHAT WE DO NOT SEE.

HEBREWS 11:1

12

Playtime
Nursery
Rhyme

Playtime Nursery Rhyme

You're absolutely gorgeous,
You're so much fun,
You're the Lord of the Years
And the King of the Deep,
But in twenty two minutes
I'm laying you down to sleep.

I love the way you gurgle
And I adore your little smile.
I know you're on a mission
And you're the chosen one,
But right now I'm going to drum
My little brown fingers
On your little round tum.

Oh, Yeshuah, Yeshuah,
I know you'll save Israel
And the whole world too,
Lead us out of slavery,
Make our stone hearts new,
But am I not of all women
Unimaginably blessed?

It's me who tickles your tiny toes
And me who nuzzles your nuzzley nose
And me who cradles you at my breast
And watches your little eyelids
Flutter as you rest.
Why me, little one,
I wonder, do you know?
Because, son of God, son of Joe,
You're my son
And I'm your mum.

12

'From now on all generations will call me blessed, for the Mighty One has done great things for me – holy is his name.'

MARY, LUKE 1:48-49

13

What
Herod
Knew

What Herod Knew

He,
Who had already killed a brother,
A wife, a son and then another,
And then another,
And found a certain peace,
He knew the dread power
Of an idea to wrench
The mind from ordinary ways.

But the travellers,
With a star in their eye
And their tale of a king,
He found quaint,
Sending them south to the predicted place,
And waiting for their disappointed return.
Then long year long he pondered their
absence,
Knowing that seekers may make truth of
coincidence.

He knew
A child will grow;
That innocence may turn to threat;
That hope may storm
The empire of the heart;
That the wind may blow
A seed to a hilltop death.

He knew.
And just to make sure
Suffered the little innocents
Spiked on his rebel crown,
And found a certain peace.

He knew,
And would rather have
killed him in the womb.
We, too late for that,
and with no taste for blood,
Would simply drown the rumour of an
empty tomb.

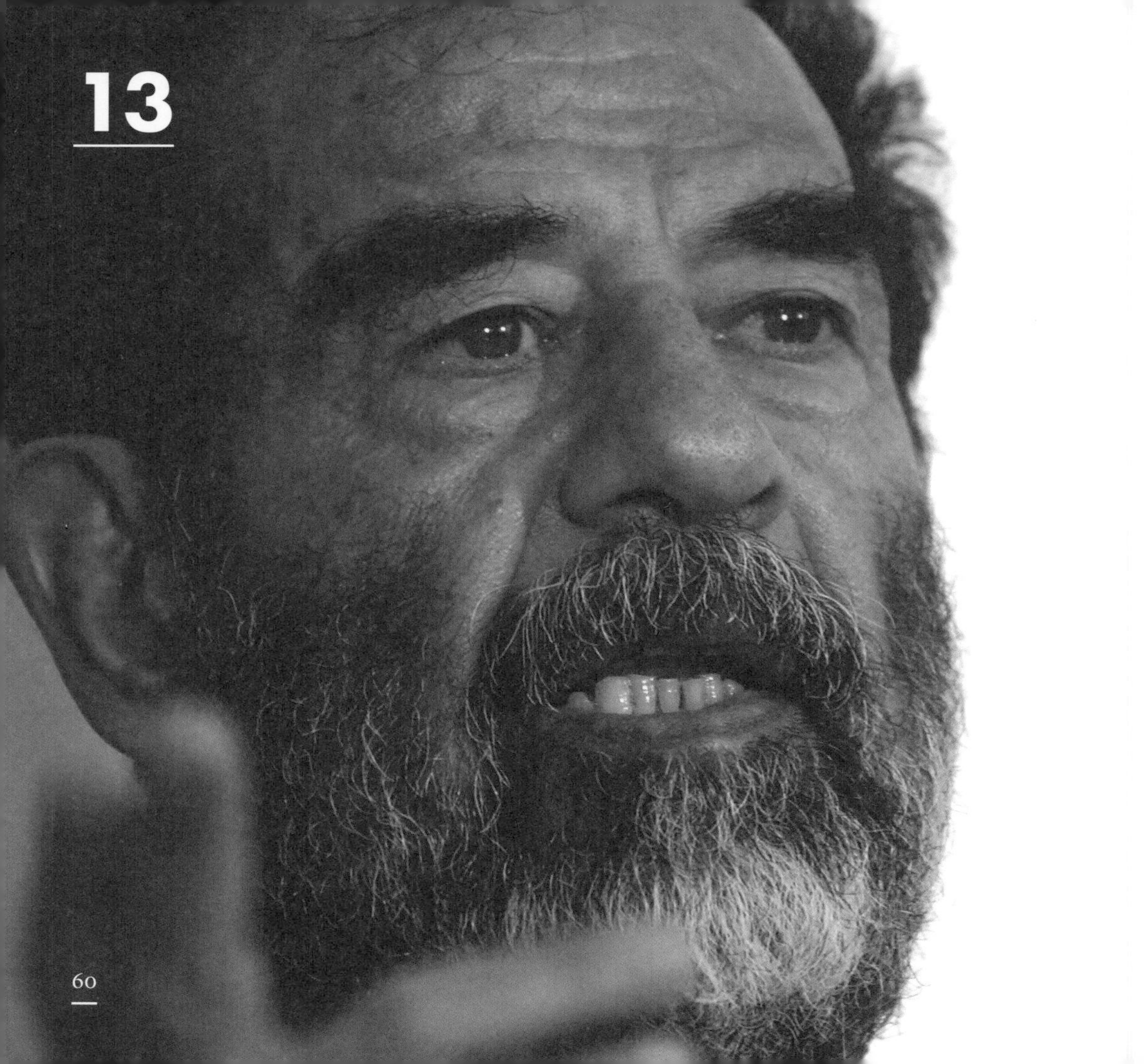

13

Yesterday, Hussein Kamel and Saddam Kamel, the sons-in-law of Saddam Hussein were murdered soon after returning to Iraq with Saddam's guarantee of safety.

The Times, February 1986

When Herod realized that he had been outwitted by the Magi, he was furious, and he gave orders to kill all the boys in Bethlehem and its vicinity who were two years old and under, in accordance with the time he had learned from the Magi.

MATTHEW 2:16

Herod the Great ruled the Province of Palestine from 37 to 4 BC. He has been described as the greatest builder in Jewish history, responsible, amongst other structures, for the rebuilding of the Temple and the mountain palace fortress at Masada. Contemporary historical documents confirm the picture we have in the Bible: Herod was a paranoid and ruthless ruler, and the serial murderer of many of his sons, his wife Mariamne, and indeed anyone who he thought might threaten his throne.

14

Kings

Kings

We were not three.
And not kings.
At least not when we arrived.
And really more curious than wise,
Craning for truth in starlit skies.
But at least looking,
At least checking
What we thought we knew:
A king born for the Jews.

No, we were not wise.
More stupid than wise,
Asking another king
To point us to a rival's cradle.
But at least asking,
And finding truth in the old scroll,
Truth a murderer would not recognise,
But wary to ply us with winsome lies
And play a deferential role.

No, we were not so wise.
More blind than wise,
Searching for a king
For someone else.
But at least searching,
And finding, in someone else's king,
Our end, the end of lifeless ways,
The rule for all our days.

Later they fancied us kings.
In that, there was only this truth:
He who would wear a crown
Must first bow low,
Must first bow down.

... and the star they had seen when it rose went ahead of them until it stopped over the place where the child was. When they saw the star, they were overjoyed.

MATTHEW 2:9–10

Every day millions of people look to the stars for guidance, hope and purpose, scanning their horoscope in a daily paper or having it beamed to their phone. The Bible bans astrology but that doesn't mean that God does not speak through his creation or that he will not turn even a misplaced enthusiasm into a stepping stone to the truth ... the seeker finds, the seeker will be found.

15

Herod's
Song

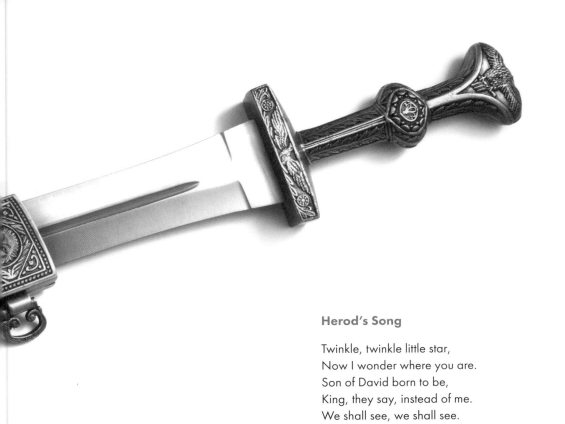

Herod's Song

Twinkle, twinkle little star,
Now I wonder where you are.
Son of David born to be,
King, they say, instead of me.
We shall see, we shall see.

15

Magi from the East came to Jerusalem and asked, 'Where is the one who has been born king of the Jews? We saw his star when it rose and have come to worship him.' When King Herod heard this he was disturbed, and all Jerusalem with him.

MATTHEW 2:1–2

We should never underestimate how far those in power will go to protect their position, their autonomy, their independence – Saddam Hussein's murder of his sons-in-law in Iraq, Nixon's attempt to cover-up the Watergate break-in in the US, Assad's brutality in Syria, Mugabe's repression in Zimbabwe, Putin's serial manipulation of the electoral system in Russia …

Herod found himself confronted by the claims of a rival king. So do we.

16

Little lamb

'Look, the lamb of God who
takes away the sin of the world!'

JOHN THE BAPTIST AT BETHANY
JOHN 1:29

Little Lamb

Mary
had a
little
lamb
His heart was pure as snow
And
though
he
loved
us
very
much
We
told
him
where
to go.

17

Joe

Joe

Others fire our imagination more swiftly.

The Magi, determined travellers from an exotic land; the angel Gabriel, fearsome and gentle, bearer of a message from the court of God; Mary, young, vulnerable, and singing out words that will resound forever.

And then there's Joseph. Honest, solid Joe.

The man in the background. Older than Mary, in the paintings at least. Old enough almost to be her father – the protector, not the lover, of a young bride.

But there's Joe ushering the donkey along the road; there's Joe being turned away by the innkeepers; there's Joe watching the travellers offer their gifts. No prophetic songs soar from his heart. The Bible records not a single word from his lips and he slips out of the story without even a sentence to mark his passing.

He's a carpenter, a working man. God didn't choose a rabbi or a scribe or a Pharisee or a rich merchant or a king to father his son, but Joe. A man who did not need an angel to appear to him to change the direction of his life, but only a dream. A man who put God's agenda for his betrothed before his own hopes. A man who left his home and his business for the sake of the girl he loved and the God he loved. A man who set aside the sexual expression of his love for Mary until after Jesus' birth, just as his son would set aside the joys of marriage for a greater love. A man who risked Herod's murderous intent and was ready to lay down his life for his bride, just as his son would risk the murderous plot of priests and people and was indeed ready to lay down his life for his bride – the church.

Maybe Jesus learned a thing or two from honest, solid Joe.

Of course, today we prefer our heroes articulate, powerful and sparkling,

'He was a righteous man,' the Bible says, an accolade it confers on very, very few people.

Good old Joe.

17

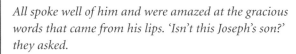

All spoke well of him and were amazed at the gracious words that came from his lips. 'Isn't this Joseph's son?' they asked.

LUKE 4:22

18

One Move Ahead

One Move Ahead

Probably he wouldn't have gone otherwise,
He, a good man, and his girl
Defiled, it seemed, by another man's smile.
But the voice in the dream
Sharp and sure
Like the words in the scroll
Told a different story:
She is pure, she is pure.

Probably he wouldn't have gone otherwise,
He, a good man, and his bride
Eight months or so with child.
Not that far, at least.
Two weeks along the hard, uneven road,
The donkey bumping and jerking
its bulging load.

But great Caesar Augustus,
For reasons of his own,
He supposed, chose this time
To number the mortals
Under his divine throne,

Sending each to register
In their natal home.

So they went.
Perhaps for a while surprised
That the Almighty should require
Such discomfort of his chosen.

But along the hard, uneven road,
Pondering an angel's words,
She, whose humility conceived a
king in her womb,
Perhaps did not worry that the journey
Would bring the child too soon.
And he, whose will had been overturned by
a dream,
Must have marvelled at the elegance of the
divine scheme:
The Lord who had trumped
the imperial decree
Would wait til they came to
the appointed place:

Son of Joseph in Joseph's town
Son of David come for his crown.

Perhaps he wouldn't have gone otherwise,
He, a good father, and his wife
So recently a mother,
And the child so small,
When the voice came again:
And this of blood on Herod's mind.

But the starmen had been and left
Gold, frankincense and myrrh,
Portable gifts, easily turned to food
and shelter.
And were they not fully equipped
And the distance already half done
For the desert road down,
Down, down to alien Egypt.

He, they realised,
was always one move ahead.

18

But after he had considered this, an angel of the Lord appeared to him in a dream and said, 'Joseph son of David, do not be afraid to take Mary home as your wife, because what is conceived in her is from the Holy Spirit.

MATTHEW 1:20

About virginity before marriage, our society knows not its mind. 51% of British people believe it's preferable to abstain from sex before marriage but 92% have had sex. Virginity is seen by some as laudable, particularly, hypocritically, in girls, but anyone of either gender who actually declares that they have decided not to have sex before marriage is seen as odd, dysfunctional, nuts – 'You cannot be serious!'

How hard then for us to grasp the high value that the Bible puts on purity, on preserving the treasure of sexual intimacy, as well as the lifelong devotion of our heart, as a gift for just one person. How hard to imagine the potentially devastating impact of her humanly inexplicable pregnancy on Mary's reputation or on her fiancé Joseph's heart. She risks all. Joseph suffers much. The road less travelled is not necessarily an easy one.

As the crow flies, it is about 80 miles from Nazareth in the North down to Bethlehem, but as the donkey walks it's further – about 100 miles. Today, it's not a particularly swift journey even by car – with all the check points and so on. Back then, it would have taken at least four days on foot or by donkey. Bethlehem, which means 'house of bread', is set on a hill, 2543 feet above sea level. And Jerusalem is about six miles to the North, on a slightly lower set of hills. We don't know where Mary and Joseph went in Egypt but it was about 75 miles from Bethlehem to the Egyptian border and around 200 miles from Bethlehem to the Nile's fertile and more populated shores.

White
Christmas

White Christmas

Some dreams may come true:

    Chestnuts roasting on an open fire,
    The soothing cool of Mediterranean blue,
    The rustling shimmer of wedding white.

The old seer's dream,
His eye scoured of fanciful self-delusion,
Saw this:

    A cedar hacked to a stump,
    Springing to a new shoot;

The village virgin's impossible boy
Crowned universal king;

The innocent prince pinned
Against the protesting sky
By the dark insistent lie
Of his adulterous bride.

This dream,
Sure in its renewed proposal,
    The eternal breeze whispering our name,
    The desert heart fountaining with joy,

This dream,
    Real in her expectant womb,
    Real in the blooded planks of that severed tree
    And the blast-bright fullness of his empty tomb,

This dream

Came true.

'A shoot will come up from the stump of Jesse;
* from his roots a Branch will bear fruit.*
The Spirit of the Lord will rest on him – '

ISAIAH WRITING CIRCA 740 BC.
ISAIAH 11:1–2

Promises, promises. There was a time when deals were sealed with a handshake, and a man's word, and a woman's too, was his bond.

Today promises have lost their currency – in too many realms too many are broken – in political manifestos, in marriage partnerships, in economic forecasts, in everyday conversation... 'I'll call you back.' How are the mighty fallen. But God's forecasts keep on coming true. Moses in the 14th century BC, David in the 11th, Isaiah and Micah in the 8th, and Daniel in the 6th point to a coming Messiah to be born in a particular place with a particular lineage to accomplish a task beyond human capacity.

20

John

John

There he was:
A signpost in camel's hair,
Right out in the middle of nowhere,
Straight, with his arm like an arrow, pointing 'There.'

I hadn't asked.
But no one goes to nowhere
If they aren't looking for somewhere.
I looked around.

'Don't look, turn.
The axe is coming.
And it means death.'
I followed the line of his arm.

In the distance, a single sheep
On the curve of a mound.
'Lost,' I said, 'A lion will get him.'
'Or it will get you.'

20

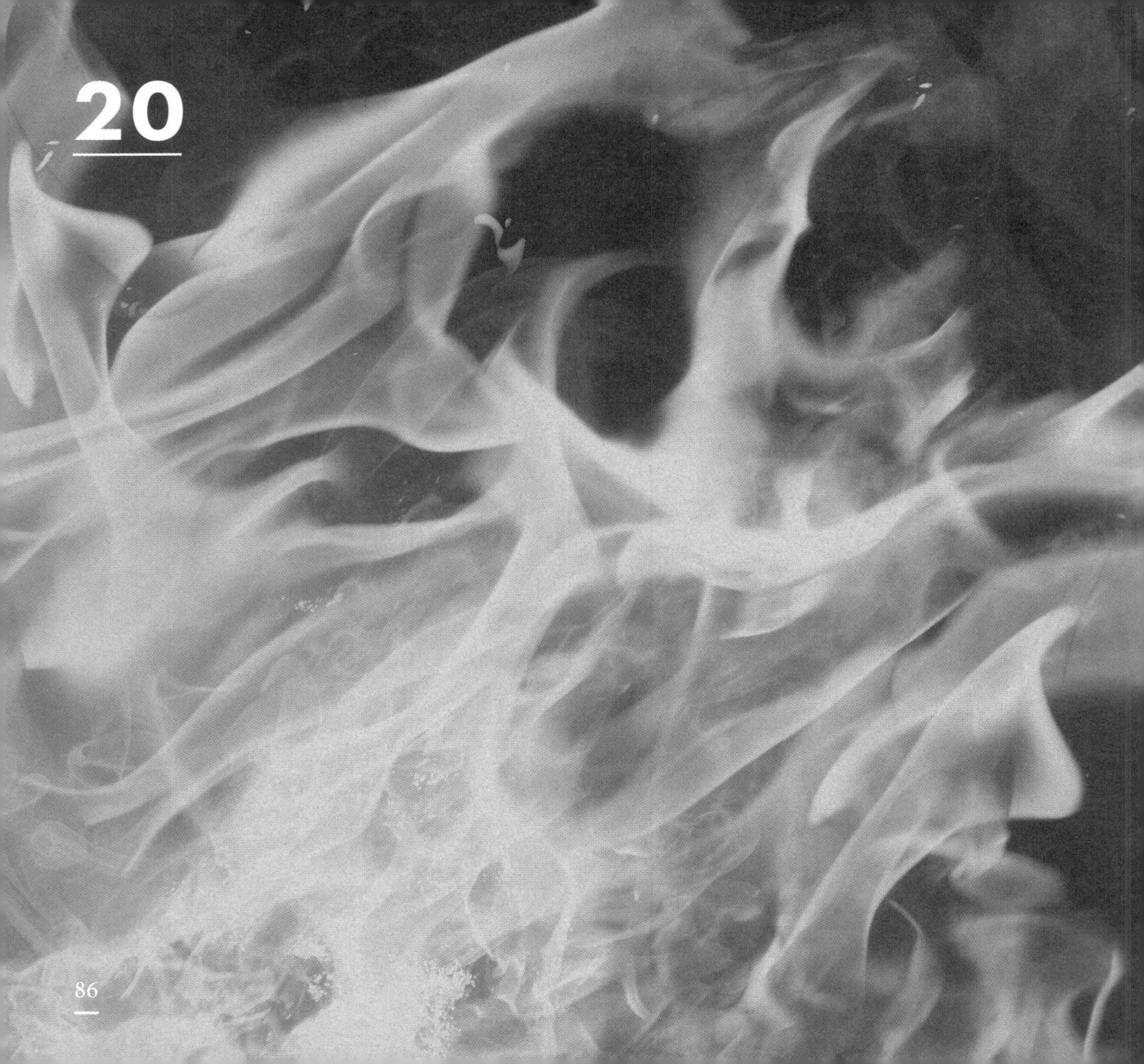

'Produce fruit in keeping with repentance … The axe has been laid to the root of the trees, and every tree that does not produce good fruit will be cut down and thrown into the fire.'

JOHN THE BAPTIST
MATTHEW 3:8, 10

Loud and proud, our culture is constantly making sure I know all about the consequences of pretty much everything in my physical and emotional worlds – from my choice of car to the impact of a particular balsamic vinegar on a rocket and mango salad. We are, however, much less comfortable even broaching the consequences of our spiritual beliefs. John wasn't. Nor was Jesus. Everyone is invited – but there comes a time when the door is shut. 'Come in quick,' they tell us.

21

Simeon

Simeon

Of a morning
The ancient breeze would unfurl,
Gentle on the old man.
Together they would go
To the place of promise.

And promise had been made,
Nested in his heart,
And promise had lain there,
Content for the future.
Only occasionally, as the years blew by,
Gusted by anxiety, he would wonder:
'Will he be, will he be?'

On this day,
The breeze, fresh and damp,
A herald of fresh rain,
Nipped his heels and scurried him on
To the customary place,

His legs aching by strange compulsion
His eye seeking some horizon...

A man, a pair of pigeons, a woman,
And a baby.

Promise soared,
A branch of olive in his lips:

'At last, here is
Word of my word,
Breath of my breath,
Life of my life.'

And breeze and breath whispered back:
'This is he, this is he.'

21

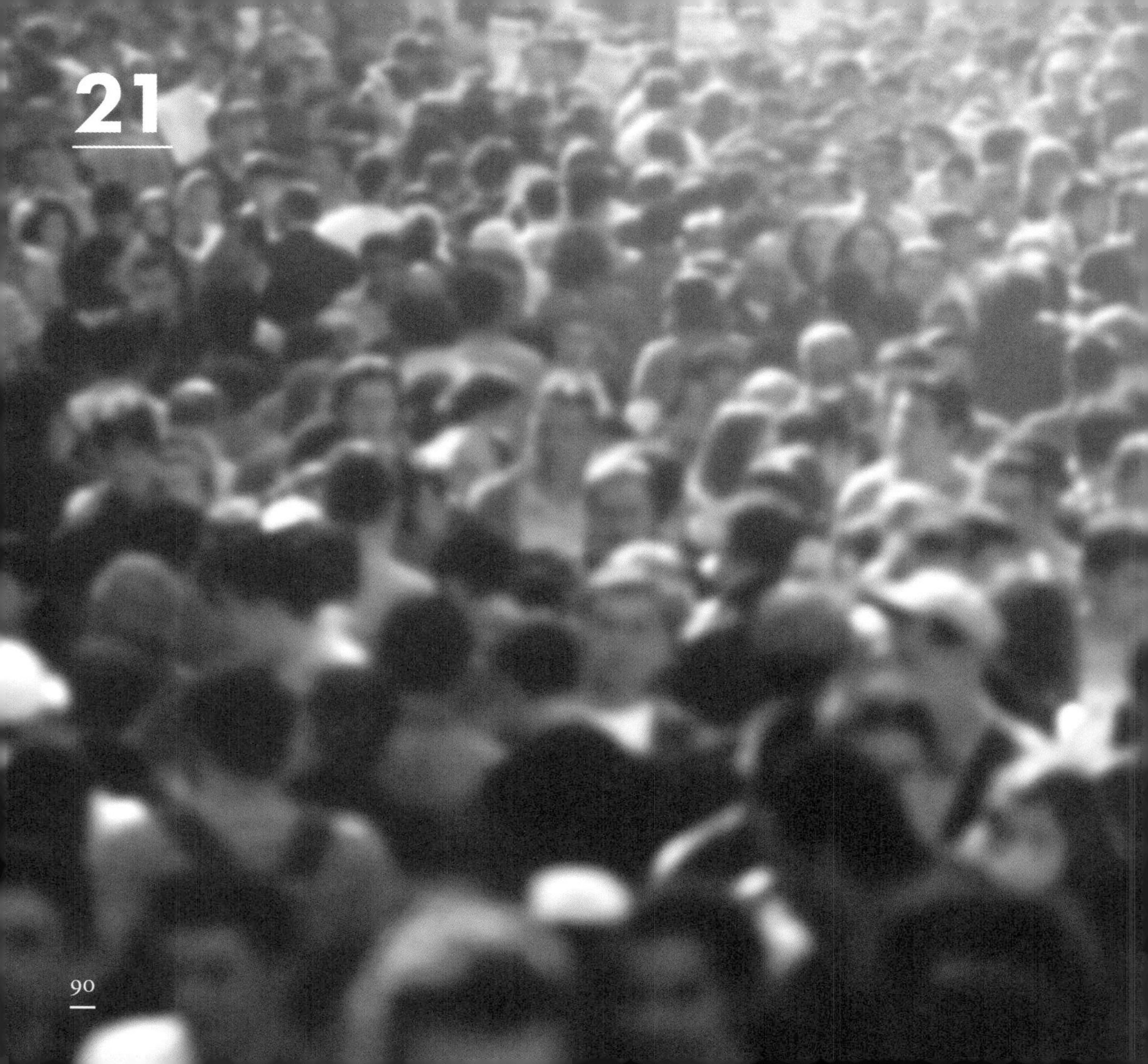

Moved by the Spirit, he went into the temple courts.

LUKE 2:27

The Temple in Jerusalem was more like a busy railway station than a hushed cathedral. Thousands visited daily, praying and making sacrifices. And at the big festivals, over 800,000 visitors would crowd the city. By comparison, around 145,000 people pass through London's King's Cross station every day.

I have a particular affection for this poem. I remember where I wrote it which I don't really recall for any of the others. And I remember how it came to me which I also don't really recall for any of the others. I was sitting on a garden chair on the tree-rich banks of the lake in Finland where my in-laws, like many Finns, have a summer cabin. It was towards the end of a warm summer day, perhaps just turning cool. In my mind's eye I can see the wind ruffling the water into little curls. And I can see the trees on the far, far shore spiking serratedly into an oceanic sky. Unusually, I suppose, because many a poem just comes, I found myself thinking about writing something about Simeon and praying specifically that God would touch it. And so, perhaps not surprisingly, when I've read this poem out loud for people, something happens: the atmosphere changes, there's a kind of hushed attention, as if the room is on pause... I'm not saying that it's a great poem, just that God touches it, just as perhaps he touches many of the ordinary things we do... and makes more of them than we ever could.

22

There

There

In the glimmer of a smile
on a care-worn face
In the fountain fresh hope of a first embrace

There

When sun sparkles on the dancing foam
And laughter splashes like the hearts
of home

There

In the pain and confusion and tears
The muffled screams and nameless fears

There

In the scuttling panic of a wind-whipped leaf
In the brimming ache of endless grief

There

In the emptiness of alone
In the grey barren of chilled stone

There

Always there

The eye brighter than the gleaming crown
The heart softer than the purple gown
The servant on the throne
The king who would be known

For no reason, except to give
In every season that we might live.

'The virgin will conceive and give birth to a son, and they will call him Immanuel'
(which means 'God with us').

MATTHEW 1:23

A while back I was in Northern Ireland at the time of The Troubles and I met a man who used to accompany the police when they'd go to someone's home to tell them that their husband or father or son had been killed. He told me this: 'No one ever remembers what anyone said, but everyone remembers who was there.'

23

Oh my God

Oh my God

Oh my God,
My God indeed,
Creator of infinite space,
Come to this God-forechosen place,
Majesty, omnipotence, glory,
Distilled in this newborn grace.

How can it be,
This your contradictory singularity?
God and man
Shepherd and lamb.
Prince and peasant
Saviour and sacrifice.
Potentate and refugee
One and three.

Oh my God,
My God indeed,
Sole seed of divine purity
Come in mortal humility to bleed
For all our sin-stained need.
Oh my God, my God in deed...

Come to me. Come to me...

*When he heard that it was Jesus of Nazareth, he began to shout,
'Jesus, Son of David, have mercy on me!'*

BARTIMAEUS, THE BLIND BEGGAR, MARK 10:47

24

Christmas Present

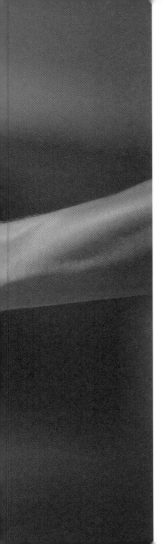

Christmas Present

On this day
Give me this to give:

Some clue to speed a traveller's way
Some myrrh to sweeten death's decay
Some gold to feed a hungry child
Some word to bring me reconciled
Some balm to soothe an aching fear
Some smile to blossom through the year
Some hope to move the will to right
Some touch to give the shuttered sight
Some power to restrain the selfish knife
Some fragrance of that future life.

On this day
Give me this to give
As you gave to me
And more.

'It is more blessed to give than to receive.'

PAUL QUOTING JESUS.

ACTS 20:35

What was the best Christmas present you ever got? I certainly remember the one I most wanted. I was about ten years old and every day for about two months on my way home from school I'd press my nose against the toyshop window. And I'd gaze in wonder at a Scalextric set and the sleek, red Jaguar D-type that I so hoped I would get to steer round sharp turns and gun down long straights to glorious victory. Still, I think the present that most moved me was from my father. It was a book. It would have cost less than £5 at the time, probably less than £10 now. It was about Islamic art – a little introduction with lots of pictures. Just right for someone with a bit of interest and no knowledge. But it wasn't the content that made it so memorable but rather that, about six months earlier, I'd casually mentioned that I'd quite like to read something about Islamic art. And he'd listened, taken note, remembered, gone looking and here it was... a book, yes, but an unforgettable tangible expression of his love for me. It is, as in all things, the love that counts.

25

Invitation

Yet to all who did receive him, to those who believed in his name, he gave the right to become children of God – children born not of natural descent, nor of human decision or a husband's will, but born of God.

JOHN 1:12–13

Invitation

To her, the invitation came, skyborne on angel's wings,
Heaven sent and pregnant with impossibilities.
For, God knows, she had reasons to say 'No',
Her future, til then, so serenely assured:
A home, her good name, a husband to wed,
Everything indeed for which she thought she'd been bred.

Are such so easily cast aside?
Would love, security, reputation
Be so swiftly pried
From our determined grasp?
How other people's risks seem simpler to take,
Our own stubborn knots so much harder to break.

To us, the royal invitation also comes,
Though usually in less spectacular script,
Sans seraph, but daily clear, which way will we go?
Of course, we are free to decline,
But 'No', promising more for now, always leads to less,
Better, braver, wiser, surely, to simply say...